501 Ways to Boost Your Child's Self-Esteem

SECOND EDITION

ROBERT D. RAMSEY, ED.D.

Contemporary Books

Chicago New York San Francisco Lisbon London Madrid Mexico City
Milan New Delhi San Juan Seoul Singapore Sydney Toronto

The **McGraw·Hill** Companies

Library of Congress Cataloging-in-Publication Data

Ramsey, Robert D.
    501 ways to boost your child's self-esteem / Robert D.
Ramsey.—2nd ed.
        p.   cm.
    ISBN 0-07-140989-0 (alk. paper)
    1. Self-esteem in children.   2. Child rearing.   I. Title:
Five hundred one ways to boost your child's self-esteem.   II.
Title: Five hundred and one ways to boost your child's self-
esteem.   III. Title.

BF723.S3 R36   2002
649'.1—dc21

                                        2002074084

Cover and interior illustrations copyright © EyeWire, Inc.
Interior design by Susan H. Hartman.

    3   4   5   6   7   8   9   0   DSH/DSH   0   1   0   9   8

ISBN 0-07-140989-0

McGraw-Hill books are available at special quantity discounts to use as
premiums and sales promotions, or for use in corporate training
programs. For more information, please write to the Director of Special
Sales, Professional Publishing, McGraw-Hill, Two Penn Plaza, New York,
NY 10121-2298. Or contact your local bookstore.

This book is printed on acid-free paper.

Contents

Introduction

How children see themselves shapes how they engage the world. One of the biggest differences between winners and losers is that winners believe in themselves and see themselves as worthy of being in the winner's circle.

Helping children to like themselves and to have a positive self-image is one of the greatest gifts any parent can bestow. Positive self-esteem is a key to successful living.

The perfect parent doesn't exist. But parents in any kind of family can find ways to help their children accept and respect themselves, believe they are "enough," and face life on equal terms.

Children don't invent a low self-esteem. They learn it from adults, mostly parents. In working with thousands of families in three major school systems in two different states, I've observed first-hand the power of positive parenting.

As the most significant influence in the lives of children, it is our job to help them experience success, make mistakes without shame, and grow up proud of who they are. This is what happens when we show them they are important, unique, special, and capable of winning in school and in life.

Raising children right is mostly a matter of doing lots of little things right. This mini-book of practical ideas that any parent can use can help you raise your children to be successful adults. These simple acts of encouragement and empowerment have worked in many families. They can work for you too.

No parent can do everything right. But any parent can do lots of right things to establish his or her child's sense of self-worth. Through caring, listening, praising, reinforcing, and taking your child seriously, you can give the gift of self-esteem and make your child a winner. The following suggestions will start you on the road. Why not begin the journey now?

1

Getting Started

1.

Start your child off right. Don't give her a silly name or initials that will cause a lifetime of embarrassment.

2.

Hug your child every day.

3.

Save the best twinkle in your eye for your child.

4.

Catch your child being good.

5.

Don't expect consistency, logic, unselfishness, or other miracles from a small child.

6.

Sometimes when there's a conflict between work and family, choose family.

7.

Don't spend much time on "what ifs" and "if onlys" in raising your child.

8.

Really listen to your child. Don't interrupt or finish his sentences. Pay attention to all the words and the feelings behind them. Real listening is a lot more than just being quiet, waiting your turn to speak.

9.

When your child needs comforting, don't worry about messing up your hair or wrinkling your clothes.

10.

Show your child positive ways to calm down.

11.

Make a big deal of birthdays. They commemorate the gift of a new life.

12.

Don't expect every lesson to be learned the first time.

13.

Spend as much time as you can outdoors with your child. Bonding flourishes in the fresh air.

14.

Listen to your child's nightmares.

15.

Show respect for your child's favorite stuffed toy.

16.

Don't end the day with an argument.

17.

Accept that it's OK not to be a perfect parent. It will reduce pressure on both you and your child.

18.

Don't always bring work home. It gives the impression that your job is more important than your family.

19.

Realize that sometimes your child cries for good reason and sometimes just for the effect.

20.

Realize that even little people can be
brokenhearted sometimes.

21.

Always give your child a second chance.

22.

When he's little, interrupt whatever
you're doing and tuck your child into
bed every night.

23.

Don't get hung up on what's "normal" for children your child's age.

24.

Don't treat all your children exactly
alike. They don't all need the same
things.

25.

Observe and listen to your child at play
to pick up clues as to how he views
himself and you.

26.

Don't count on popular women's
magazines to help raise your child.

27.

Encourage your child to try again.

28.

Get down on eye level with your child once in a while.

29.

Don't take yourself too seriously as a parent. A lot of good growing up will occur in spite of you.

30.

Rock your child a lot when she is tiny. It empowers both of you.

31.

Pick wildflowers with your child.

32.

Let your child play with your pots and pans once in a while.

33.

Discipline with firmness—not with anger.

34.

Talk to other parents a lot. Don't raise your child in a vacuum.

35.

Remember, not all bruises show up on the outside.

36.

If you can't think of the right words to say, just hold your child close. That says it all.

37.

Don't tease your child if it's not fun for her.

38.

Celebrate your child's successes—even little ones.

39.

Appreciate a dandelion bouquet if you're lucky enough to get one.

40.

Remember that sometimes being a parent is about loving the unlovable.

41.

Write down the whimsical and funny things your child says. They'll entertain your family for years to come.

42.

Leave a light on if your child is afraid of the dark.

43.

Establish routines. They add to your child's sense of security.

44.

Don't make every meal a contest of wills. Give in sometimes. (Remember the president who didn't like broccoli?)

45.

Don't act concerned if your little girl is a tomboy or if your little boy likes to play with dolls. Little children shouldn't have to live up to adults' preconceived notions of what kids are supposed to like and do.

46.

Let your child play dress-up in your old clothes.

47.

Be sure to fill in all of your child's baby book. You'll both enjoy it in future years.

48.

Despite the protests of dentists and nutritionists, remember that every child needs candy once in a while.

49.

Never say never. It's come back to haunt many parents.

50.

Make special pancakes on Sunday morning.

51.

If feasible, name godparents for your child. It enlarges the child's lifelong support group.

52.

Don't get in the habit of comparing your child with everyone else's.

53.

Teach your child the difference between "me first" and "my turn."

54.

Be satisfied with your child as he is.

55.

Save something important from each year of your child's life.

56.

Let grandparents spoil your child. That's what grandmas and grandpas are for.

57.

Take time to have a tea party with your child while she is still small.

58.

Avoid "do it or else" situations whenever possible.

59.

Ride an old-fashioned merry-go-round with your child.

60.

Have favorite books that you
read and reread to your child.
(Dr. Seuss is always a good choice.)

61.

Let your child hold the new baby.

62.

If there's a problem with potty-training,
don't make your child feel like a bad
person.

63.

Don't let your child be a tyrant at home. It's unfair to everyone in the family, including the child.

64.

Listen to crickets chirping at nightfall with your child.

65.

Let your child watch baby birds hatch or puppies being born.

66.

Make it a point to show your children you love them the first thing every morning and the last thing every night.

67.

Select your child's day care or preschool as carefully as you pick out a new car.

68.

Laugh with your children and cry with them too.

69.

Don't worship at the "altar of what other people think" in raising your children.

70.

Don't slack off taking photos or completing baby books with your second or third child. It gives the impression that the firstborn is the most important.

71.

Do more bragging than nagging.

72.

Never be embarrassed to say
"I love you."

73.

Make it clear that certain behavior is
unacceptable, but that doesn't make the
person doing it unacceptable.

74.

Skip stones across water with your child.

75.

If your child makes it, cherish it.

76.

Don't expect your child to "take it like a man" if he's still a little boy.

77.

Don't rush childhood.

78.

Smile a lot. It won't crack your face and it will help break the ice with your child.

79.

Post your child's drawings and schoolwork in prominent places. That's what refrigerator doors are for.

80.

Remember, if your child thinks it's important, it's important.

81.

Recognize your child's good intentions, even though the follow-through doesn't always happen.

82.

Have family carnivals where each member has his own booth and gives out prizes from the junk drawer.

83.

Minimize shaming and blaming in your family.

84.

Remember, no child is too small to own something nice.

85.

Never forget that you are your child's first and most important teacher.

86.

Visit a pet shop with your child. Help him cultivate a love of animals.

87.

Let your child have a secret hideout.

88.

Sometimes, allow your child to eat dessert first.

89.

At least once, let your child be the "first kid on the block" to do or have something.

90.

Don't go overboard on Santa
Claus, the Easter Bunny, and the
Tooth Fairy. It can shake your
child's confidence and trust when
she learns the truth.

91.

Remember that hot chocolate on a cold day can help melt the ice and warm up conversation between you and your child.

92.

Don't pooh-pooh imaginary friends.

93.

Make a tent or fort in your living room and camp out inside some night.

94.

Expect your child to let you down
sometimes.

95.

Make sure your child gets to see a circus
sometime.

96.

Always tell your child good-bye before
you leave.

97.

Walk in a warm, soft rain together with
your child.

98.

Always answer when your child speaks to you. Being ignored makes him feel invisible.

99.

Don't make your child do or try things he is afraid of.

100.

Sing along with your child.

101.

Remember all those things you said as a child that you would never do when you grew up and had your own children—and don't do them.

2

The Primary Grades

102.

Develop family traditions. They provide predictability and stability that comforts children. Many times, children will perpetuate these same traditions as adults.

103.

Don't worry much about your child staying inside the lines when coloring.

104.

Don't always make your little children eat at a separate table when company comes.

105.

Let your child tell you a story at bedtime now and then.

106.

Don't tickle your child if it drives her crazy.

107.

Wink at your child when you two have a secret.

108.

Notice when your child does something better.

109.

Have a plan in case you get separated from your child at the mall or in a crowd.

110.

Go wading with your child and squish mud between your toes.

111.

Hold hands with your child.

112.

Build sandcastles with your child.

113.

Find a tree that both you and your child can climb.

114.

Let your child put ketchup or chocolate on anything she wants sometimes.

115.

Bake cookies together.

116.

Let your child help wash the family car.

117.

Always have a surprise on hand for those times when something good happens unexpectedly.

118.

Don't be too fussy about how clean your child's room is. Twenty years from now it won't matter much.

119.

Look for the first signs of spring with your child.

120.

Spend one-on-one time with each child every week.

121.

Resist the temptation to say, "You're too little to understand."

122.

Let your child say grace at mealtime.

123.

Don't always make your child eat the dark meat.

124.

Hunt for seashells with your child and keep the most interesting ones you find.

125.

Grow something together.

126.

Make something special on Valentine's Day. It's one of the few occasions dedicated exclusively to love.

127.

Stay home and have a family New Year's Eve party one year.

128.

Let your child pop the popcorn.

129.

Rake leaves with your child—and play in them together.

130.

If you can, arrange for your child to ride on a fire truck or in a police car.

131.

Don't act dramatically different toward your child in public than you do in private.

132.

You don't have to let your child win every time you play a game, but everyone should win sometimes.

133.

Let your children serve you breakfast in bed on your birthday, Mother's Day, or Father's Day.

134.

Watch for signs of stress in your child (bad dreams, unreasonable temper tantrums, etc.).

135.

Go to a state or county fair with your child. Visit the animal barns together.

136.

Once in a while set aside an evening for the entire family to play board games.

137.

Don't tell your child, "This will hurt me more than it will you." No kid's going to buy that story.

138.

Teach your child that everyone makes mistakes and you don't have to be perfect to be loved.

139.

When you're away, call to tell your child you miss her.

140.

Praise effort—not just success.

141.

If you can't go to the seashore, have a beach party at home around the wading pool and the sandbox.

142.

Make a mobile out of objects reflecting your child's interests.

143.

Consistently communicate an "I know you can do it" attitude to your child.

144.

Take your child on a hayride.

145.

Apologize to your child when you're wrong.

146.

Give your child her own little treasure chest with a lock and key.

147.

Let your child make fun of you sometimes.

148.

At some point, you may have to help your child understand that the world still revolves around the sun and not around him.

149.

See to it that your child learns to swim.

150.

Videotape your child's first day at school. It's one of life's major milestones.

151.

Realize that how parents treat each other is as important as how they treat their child in shaping the child's understanding of what a relationship is supposed to be.

152.

Don't miss parent-teacher
conferences.

153.

Know what your child takes to "Show and Tell" and why. It signals what your child values most.

154.

Don't make fun of your child's phobias (fear of spiders or heights, for example). It's not funny to the child.

155.

Let your child decorate her own birthday cake.

156.

If you borrow from your child, always
pay it back.

157.

Volunteer at school.

158.

If your child's pet dies, give it a dignified
funeral.

159.

Let your child know it's OK to have a bad day.

160.

Eat lunch at school with your child.

161.

Remember that eating ice cream can be good therapy for lots of ills.

162.

Fly the flag on the Fourth of July and teach your child that patriotism isn't corny.

163.

Slip an encouraging note into your child's lunch box.

164.

Call your child when you're going to be late.

165.

Don't always talk about how much you sacrifice for your child. Talk about the joy you receive in return.

166.

Whenever your child is going to a new school or camp or baby-sitter, visit with your child in advance so that she knows what to expect. It reduces fear and builds self-confidence.

167.

Pray together.

168.

Let your child pack her own suitcase for an overnight trip.

169.

Put your child's name first sometimes when you sign a letter from your family.

170.

Teach your child a secret code.

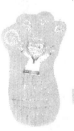

171.

Put your child's events on your family and personal calendars.

172.

Have a professional artist make a portrait of your child. You'll both cherish it for years to come.

173.

Give your child a music box that plays one of her favorite songs.

174.

When you can't get close enough
to speak to your child, give him
the thumbs-up sign.

175.

Don't stuff your feelings. It teaches your child an unhealthy coping strategy.

176.

Be proud of your child for what he doesn't do as well as for what he does.

177.

Don't let your child's acts of kindness go unnoticed.

178.

Nurture your child's talents, whatever they may be.

179.

Teach your child what it means to be a good neighbor.

180.

Help your child start her own collection of Christmas tree ornaments.

181.

Wear a locket with your child's picture in it. It shows that she is important to you.

182.

Take off work unexpectedly and do something fun with your child.

183.

Take your child to see your childhood home and neighborhood and share what it was like when you were growing up.

184.

Let your child take care of you when
you're sick (and not contagious).

185.

Teach your child how to accept a
compliment.

186.

Let your child teach you something.

187.

Let your child pick the gifts he wants to
give others.

188.

Don't take your child's worries lightly.

189.

Browse together in a bookstore.

190.

Go to a children's play together.

191.

Sometime, have a special candlelight dinner in your child's honor.

192.

Really read what your child has written.

193.

Ask your child for help sometimes.

194.

Teach your child to read the cards that accompany gifts.

195.

Let your child record the greeting message on your answering machine (subject to your review).

196.

Watch reruns of your favorite childhood TV series with your child. It gives the two of you a sense of change and a basis for comparison.

197.

Let your child have her own garden.

198.

Let your child attend the funeral of a
loved one. It helps your child
acknowledge the loss.

199.

Give your child a set of dog tags
containing full identification
information.

200.

Let your child pick out things and plan
for a new baby.

201.

"Walk the talk." Try to live up to what
you teach and preach.

202.

Use butcher paper to set up a family
graffiti wall for depicting daily
highlights.

203.

Negotiate, but don't capitulate, on important issues with your child.

204.

Give your child her own key.

205.

Always share with your child what the teacher says at conference time. Silence and secrecy feel like a conspiracy to a child.

206.

Don't pass on your fear and distrust of authority to your child.

207.

Teach your child how to plan ahead.

208.

Start a bank account in your child's name.

209.

Introduce your child to people. Don't act as if he isn't there.

210.

If your child is shy and embarrassed, shake hands in public and hug in private.

211.

Don't act as if it's only what adults do
that is important.

212.

Make mornings as calm as possible. A
frenzied start can louse up a whole day.

213.

Learn to read and respond to your
child's body language.

214.

Remember, no child should go to sleep
feeling unwanted.

215.

Use direct eye contact to show your child that he has your undivided attention.

216.

Don't let your child become a pawn in a power struggle between parents.

217.

Learn about the impact of birth order on children.

218.

Take your child seriously.

219.

Whisper to your child sometimes.
It makes her feel close and "in on"
something secretive.

220.

Don't treat your friends better than you do your child.

221.

Quit using baby nicknames when your child begins to be uncomfortable with them.

222.

Don't always be tired when your child gets home from school. Save enough energy for an enthusiastic welcome.

223.

If your child loves to draw or sing, but isn't very good at it—don't tell her.

224.

If you are gone for a period of time, leave some little surprises for your child to open each day in your absence.

225.

Name your fishing boat after your child.

226.

Let your children invent their own pizzas using whatever toppings they choose.

227.

Don't blow off your child's ideas.

228.

Don't tell your child how much you hated school.

229.

Go for a canoe ride alone with your child. It's an amazingly quiet place to talk.

230.

Resist the temptation to be first to brag about your child's successes. Let him tell others about his accomplishments before you do.

231.

Acquaint your child with traditional myths, stories, and fairy tales. It will help make her culturally literate.

232.

When a loss occurs, remember that children go through the same grief cycle as adults. Support them throughout the process.

233.

Let your child plan a birthday party for a grandparent.

234.

Don't be afraid to give your daughter karate lessons. The martial arts teach poise, grace, and self-confidence, as well as self-defense.

235.

Teach your child the difference between "good touch" and "bad touch."

236.

Learn from the wisdom of your child's grandparents. They did something right. They raised your child's parents.

237.

Don't count on the school to do your job.

238.

Allow reasonable time for improvement. Some faults can be corrected immediately; others take time in order for your child to learn new behavior.

239.

Maintain an open door policy for your children, but let them close theirs.

240.

Stress progress, not perfection, with your child.

241.

Let your child eat pizza for breakfast sometimes.

242.

Tell your child about your own dreams and hopes for the future.

243.

Don't be afraid to let your child see you cry.

244.

Make the most of what time you have with your child. Even grocery shopping can be "quality time" if you make it interesting and fun.

245.

Don't overreact to the sniffles. Hypochondria is a communicable disease.

246.

If there's trouble between parents, be sure your child understands it's not his fault.

247.

Give your child choices whenever
possible.

248.

Watch sunrises and sunsets together with
your child.

249.

Have a reason for your rules.

250.

Let your child wear wild socks if he
wants to.

251.

Help your child remember the good things she does. This is the basis of self-esteem.

252.

Don't decide what your child is like
based on an IQ or any other test score.

253.

Don't rely on bribery to get the job
done. It's not an effective tool for
parenting.

254.

Remember that children need standards
and find limits comforting and
supportive.

255.

Give your child something important to do and let him do it his own way.

256.

Have a backup plan in case something your child is counting on falls through.

257.

Give your child an old-fashioned police whistle to use as an alarm or call for help.

258.

Be on time every time for appointments with your child.

259.

If you're wrong, promptly admit it.

260.

Don't shy away from affection just because your child is growing older.

3

The Intermediate Grades

261.

Go hiking together.

262.

Don't set your children up for failure by pushing them to do things they aren't ready for.

263.

Let your child put her handprint or footprint in the wet cement of your new driveway or sidewalk.

264.

Treat your child to a root beer float for no reason.

265.

Laugh at your child's jokes.

266.

Get your child's teeth fixed if they need it. A winning smile helps build self-confidence.

267.

Be silly with your child once in a while.

268.

If your child has a favorite outfit, let her wear it—a lot.

269.

Don't spare superlatives ("Wow," "Terrific," "Awesome," etc.) when your child excels at something.

270.

Let your child use your cologne or aftershave.

271.

Spend time stargazing with your child on a still night.

272.

Don't make excuses for your child. Let her take the consequences of her actions.

273.

Understand that sometimes your child may not want to grow up. It's too scary. Let him be little a little while longer.

274.

If your child complains that you're too crabby, think about it. The kid just might be right.

275.

Walk the family dog with your child. It's a good time to talk. Walking and talking just naturally go together.

276.

Enjoy spontaneous picnics with your child.

277.

Try to buy your children gifts of equal value. They may be keeping score.

278.

Let your child "buy" his own tickets for movies and carnival rides.

279.

When your whole family goes on a trip, be sure to do some "kid stuff" part of the time.

280.

Teach your child that the only dumb question is the one never asked.

281.

Build something together with your child.

282.

If your child tells you a secret, keep it.

283.

Send your child something through the mail.

284.

Don't promise what you can't deliver.

285.

If your child catches an edible fish,
eat it.

286.

Do whatever you can to expand your
child's vocabulary.

287.

Let your child help make the weekly
grocery list.

288.

Remember the names of your child's friends.

289.

Let your child have a lemonade stand.

290.

Let your child help decide where to plant the new tree in your yard.

291.

Encourage your child to learn and try new things—but don't push too hard or too fast.

292.

Don't ignore or shy away from tough questions.

293.

Tell other people about your child's successes—in front of your child.

294.

Teach your child to finish projects once they're started.

295.

Remember what your child tells you.

296.

Encourage your child to explore and solve problems on his own, rather than you doing things for him all the time.

297.

Don't throw away something your child really wants to keep for a while longer.

298.

If you can't buy a new bike, at least paint the old one.

299.

Let your child eat off the good dishes like the grown-ups once in a while.

300.

Let your child help you with the family barbecue. Teach her the secrets of your special burgers.

301.

Let your child pick out your earrings or necktie sometimes.

302.

Hang a full-length mirror in your child's room.

303.

Make "looking out for each other" a
basic value in your family.

304.

Invite your child to visit you at work.

305.

Get your child her own magazine
subscription.

306.

Teach your child how to apologize.

307.

Let your child see you be romantic with your spouse sometimes.

308.

Take your child to an old-fashioned drive-in movie (if you can find one).

309.

When your child's world has come to an end, just help him get through the day. A new world will start tomorrow.

310.

Give your child a personalized mug.

311.

Don't be phony around your child. She'll know it and her trust will be undermined.

312.

Show your child how to break big tasks down into smaller ones and take one step at a time.

313.

Let your child know that anybody can have a good idea.

314.

Don't accept sloppy work from your child. There is pride in a job well done.

315.

Let your child name the family pet.

316.

Teach your child that the world isn't much impressed by show-offs and know-it-alls.

317.

Remember that older children don't like to be babied.

318.

Teach your child good manners. It will give her more confidence in social situations.

319.

Don't switch channels in the middle of your child's favorite program.

320.

Teach your child ways to have fun without spending money.

321.

Give your child a children's cookbook and let him try out some dishes on the whole family.

322.

Don't patronize your child. She may not know what to call it, but she'll know what you're doing and won't like it.

323.

Let your child sign the guest book at weddings and other functions.

324.

Teach your child to accept help when it's needed and offered.

325.

Let your child help with home-improvement projects.

326.

Let your child put out a family newspaper if he wants to.

327.

Buy your child something with her monogram on it.

328.

Encourage your child to start a collection that no one else has.

329.

Give your child a vacation from chores once in a while. (If it's good for you, it's good for your child.)

330.

Teach your child about the power of first impressions.

331.

Make sure your child develops the habit of writing thank-you notes.

332.

Teach your child how to read a map.

333.

Don't overschedule your child.
Give him time to be "just a kid."

334.

Get your child the autograph of someone famous or important to him.

335.

Steer your child away from video or computer games that feature violence.

336.

Have some baseball cards made with your child's picture on them.

337.

Hold brainstorming sessions to solve family problems where the children's ideas count as much as the grown-ups'.

338.

Put your child in charge of a family project such as decorating for the holidays.

339.

If you can't find the right words to say something important to your child, write it down. Who says you can't write a letter to your own children?

340.

Be sure your child has the phone numbers of relatives and close friends in case she needs help and can't reach you.

341.

Help your child put together a family time capsule to be opened on his twenty-first birthday.

342.

Teach your child that bigger isn't always better.

343.

Teach your child to take care of his own clothes. It will give both of you greater independence.

344.

Give your child some tools of her own.

345.

If your child volunteers you for
something, don't back out.

346.

Put up a volleyball or badminton net in
the backyard for family games.

347.

Have your child design a family logo.

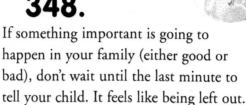

348.

If something important is going to happen in your family (either good or bad), don't wait until the last minute to tell your child. It feels like being left out.

349.

Watch the evening news with your child and help him understand what's going on in the world.

350.

Teach your child how to be alone without being lonely.

351.

Let your child decorate the door to his room as a way to express individuality.

352.

Try to get your child a musical instrument if she wants to play one.

353.

For fun, teach your child about her sign of the zodiac.

354.

Teach your child to check for accuracy.

355.

Let your child help plan the family vacation.

356.

Don't send your child off to school with lipstick on his cheek.

357.

Let your child manage some of her own money.

358.

Don't make light of your child's crush on someone else.

359.

Teach your child to read music.

360.

Don't intrude when your child is in the bathroom.

361.

Emphasize the importance of an education to a successful and fulfilling life.

362.

Encourage your child to write an illustrated autobiography. It helps validate her as a distinct individual.

363.

When it's belt-tightening time in the family, let your child suggest his own cost-cutting measures. It makes him feel a part of the team.

364.

Don't stop giving your child hugs and kisses just because you think he is getting too old for displays of affection.

365.

Save your child's ribbons, awards, and trophies.

366.

Teach your child how to sew on buttons.

367.

Don't shield your child from family problems.

368.

Teach your child how to use the
microwave oven.

369.

Never use abusive phrases such as "You
brat" or "You're no good" with your
child.

370.

Encourage your child to learn a foreign
language at an early age. Better yet, learn
it along with your child.

371.

Teach your child how to start a filing
system of her own.

372.

Give your child her own alarm clock.

373.

Have family workout sessions. Sweating
together builds stronger families as well
as stronger bodies.

374.

Put your child's name on the family
mailbox, along with your own.

375.

Have your child design a family flag—
and fly it.

376.

Teach your child to "allow enough
time."

377.

Help your child make a junk art
sculpture out of broken or discarded
toys.

378.

Don't dress your children for your tastes.
Let them dress for the real world in
which they live.

379.

Teach your child how to change a fuse
or reset a circuit breaker.

380.

Teach your child how to make
introductions.

381.

Teach your child how to count change.

382.

Have a red carpet to roll out when your child comes home after a special victory.

383.

Concoct a new recipe and name the dish after your child. Better yet, let your child invent a recipe.

384.

If possible, stay out of sibling issues. Things usually work out best when kids work them out for themselves.

385.

Watch for signs that your child may be a victim of abuse, bullying, or extortion outside the home.

386.

Make computer banners to celebrate your child's accomplishments and milestones.

387.

Let your children know they will be cared for if something happens to you.

388.

If your child does something really good, don't forget it right away.

4

Middle School/Junior High

389.

Try to attend every event, game, and performance in which your child is involved.

390.

Respect your child's privacy.

391.

Go fishing with your child.

392.

Don't try to relive your life through your child.

393.

When you're angry, don't give your child the "silent treatment." It will only tempt her to do the same to you later on.

394.

Don't hold a grudge against your child.

395.

Don't feel you always have to have the last word.

396.

Get help if you have a problem of
dependency or addiction of any kind. It
will revitalize your self-esteem and your
child's as well.

397.

Let your child know that if he needs
you, you'll be there no matter what.

398.

Remember, you're the adult.

399.

Get all the facts before dealing out any discipline.

400.

Teach your child to give herself "positive inside messages" in the face of negative peer pressure.

401.

Take care of your own needs for rest. Fatigue breeds short tempers, and tired parents tend to be overly cautious, conservative, and restrictive.

402.

Try to see your child as others see him. It may give you added respect for him.

403.

Don't use sarcasm with your child. It never works and almost always alienates.

404.

Don't try to buy your child's respect. It won't work for you and it won't work for him if he tries it on others later on.

405.

Realize that sometimes shame and embarrassment are punishment enough.

406.

Don't force your company on your child's friends. Act like a grown-up, not one of the kids.

407.

Talk to your child about her hopes for the future.

408.

Sometimes, discuss with your children, "How can we do better as a family?"

409.

Be willing to not know everything that goes on in your child's life.

410.

During the down times, challenge your child to think of all the things she likes about herself and her life.

411.

Have your child join you in helping to serve meals at a homeless shelter on Thanksgiving. It reinforces the importance of service to others.

412.

Trust your child as much as you can.

413.

Show your child the value of goal setting. It has the power to change her life.

414.

Find a sport you can play with your child.

415.

Give your child his own appointment book and daily planner.

416.

Don't go overboard in correcting your child's grammar. She may stop talking to you altogether.

417.

Pay attention to significant rites of passage (graduation, bar mitzvahs, etc.).

418.

Don't make more of your child's athletic accomplishments than you do of her academic achievements.

419.

Respect the fads and fashions of your child's generation.

420.

Help your child see through the media-inspired fantasy of a problem-free, happy-ever-after life.

421.

Encourage your child to get CPR and other first-aid training.

422.

Don't get hung up on matching mother-daughter outfits. Your child may think they are stupid and embarrassing.

423.

Don't knowingly allow your child to do
something wrong or dangerous just
because it's a hassle to say no.

424.

Make a special quilt or afghan for your
child.

425.

Don't be shocked if your children use
the same language they hear you using.

426.

Be familiar with movie, video, and rock stars your child idolizes. It helps keep you relevant in your child's eyes.

427.

Don't always answer your child's
questions with other questions.

428.

Don't put down today's music.

429.

Teach your child that the only person
she can really change is herself.

430.

Teach your child to trust his hunches, feelings, and instincts. If he senses danger, he should do something about it.

431.

Teach your child what the word "compromise" means.

432.

Help your child count her blessings. Most of us are better off than we think we are.

433.

Encourage your child to set some
goals that are not easily reached.
We all need to stretch at times.

434.

Help your child understand the physical changes of adolescence.

435.

Make a "Welcome Home" banner for your child's return from camp or a trip.

436.

Debunk the media myth that the world is made up of thin, perfectly proportioned people.

437.

Reinforce the value of a healthy lifestyle for your child.

438.

Encourage your child to keep a journal.

439.

Don't give too much advice. Kids become immune to it after a while.

440.

Help your child learn about "natural highs."

441.

If your child is concerned about being overweight, don't shrug it off. Help her learn about proper diet and exercise.

442.

Act your age if you expect your child to act his.

443.

Tell your child what to do about obscene phone calls.

444.

Remember, it's not inconceivable for a child to win an argument with an adult sometimes. Even an adolescent can be right once in a while.

445.

Encourage your child to "take a bow inside" when she succeeds.

446.

See to it that your child learns to dance.

447.

Give your child punishment
options where appropriate.

448.

Look the other way sometimes.

449.

Don't always call your son "Junior."

450.

For a special treat, surprise your child with a "4-Star Hotel" bed turndown service, complete with a chocolate on her pillow.

451.

Be willing to consider extenuating circumstances.

452.

Don't make your child feel that you're watching him all the time.

453.

Remember that, sometimes, the best thing a parent can do is shut up.

454.

When things are bad on the streets, don't let the streets into your home. Home is one haven every child should be able to count on.

455.

Have the family give your child a standing ovation when she deserves it.

456.

If all the other kids really are doing it, reconsider your "No."

457.

Remember, no one is ever too old for "warm fuzzies."

458.

Teach your child it's better to solve problems than to assign blame.

459.

Don't take good behavior for granted. Kids (like adults) deserve credit for doing what they are supposed to do.

5

High School and Beyond

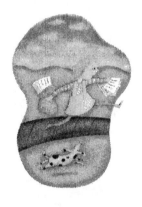

460.

Be optimistic. It's catching.

461.

Don't draw a line in the sand during a sandstorm. You shouldn't pick the worst possible time to take a stand.

462.

Help your child remember the good times in the bad times.

463.

Don't lie to your child—but don't lie for her either.

464.

Be quick to forgive.

465.

Don't make guilt a big part of your child's life.

466.

Tell your child the truth—always say what you mean and mean what you say.

467.

No matter how busy everyone gets, find time to eat meals together as a family on a regular basis.

468.

If you want to take some credit for your child's successes, be willing to take part of the blame for his failures.

469.

Sometimes on a special occasion, give your child a gift certificate and let him pick out his own present.

470.

Have your child plan and produce a home video of your family.

471.

If you absolutely can't attend one of your child's important games or performances, try to arrange for someone else (grandparent, friend, neighbor, etc.) to be present for support. Every child, no matter how old, needs at least one fan in the stands.

472.

End each year by reviewing the past twelve months of individual and family accomplishments.

473.

Don't presume your child will follow in your footsteps.

474.

Show your child how you budget your income and save for "big-ticket" items.

475.

Give your child a T-shirt or sweater from your alma mater.

476.

Occasionally, show up at your child's practice—not just for the Big Game.

477.

Always leave a light on for your child when she is out at night.

478.

As your child grows older, let go and get more of a life of your own. Allow your child to do the same.

479.

Establish a curfew. There will be times when your child will welcome an excuse to get home "on time."

480.

Stop calling them kids when they're teenagers.

481.

Know what classes your teen is taking in school and who the teachers are.

482.

Expect some backtalk from your high schooler. It's part of finding out how to be independent.

483.

Appreciate that acne is a serious social affliction for teenagers.

484.

Don't try to dress, look, or act as young as your teenager.

485.

Don't try to pick your child's career for her. Encourage and support her choices.

486.

Be concerned if your high school student doesn't rebel a little. Growing up requires a bit of tension between parents and children.

487.

Promise to pick up your child anywhere, anytime when drinking is involved—no questions asked.

488.

Never give up trying to be a good parent.

489.

Get to know your child's employer and what your child does at work.

490.

Expect your child to nag you about your bad habits (smoking, not exercising, not recycling, not using seat belts, etc.). Once in a while, let your child change your behavior and give her credit for your improvement.

491.

Admonish your child to never go anywhere with anyone he doesn't know or trust.

492.

Tell your child, "I like you." It's different from "I love you," but it's just as important at any age.

493.

Let your child know it's OK not to have everything figured out. Even adults have self-doubts.

494.

Be yourself. Being a parent isn't supposed to be an act.

495.

Don't overglamorize your youth. Admit you weren't always perfect either.

496.

Be on your best behavior when your child is trying to impress someone.

497.

Don't expect your child to solve your problems.

498.

Make it comfortable for your child to
have friends over.

499.

Don't do things for your teenagers that
they can do for themselves. It's called
growing up.

500.

Teach your child the Serenity Prayer
from Alcoholics Anonymous. Its message
will serve him well.
"God, grant me the serenity
to accept the things I cannot change;
courage to change the things I can;
and wisdom to know the difference."

501.

Don't be too quick to take over or give away your child's room when she goes away to school or work.

"All too often we are giving our young people cut flowers when we should be teaching them to grow their own plants."

—John W. Gardner

About the Author

Dr. Robert D. Ramsey is a lifelong educator and freelance writer from Minneapolis. His professional career includes extensive frontline experience in three award-winning school districts in two different states as a teacher, counselor, supervisor, curriculum coordinator, personnel director, associate superintendent, acting superintendent, and adjunct professor.

Dr. Ramsey is the author of several successful books for parents and educators and a frequent contributor to numerous popular journals and newspapers.

Most important, he is a father and grandfather.